SUFFOLK MOODS

David Gynn

HALSGROVE

First published in Great Britain in 2006

Title page photograph: *Colourful clouds are mirrored in the calmness of the River Stour at dawn.*

British Library Cataloguing-in-Publication Data
A CIP record for this title is available from the British Library

ISBN 1 84114 555 6
ISBN 978 1 84114 555 6

HALSGROVE
Halsgrove House
Lower Moor Way
Tiverton, Devon EX16 6SS
Tel: 01884 243242
Fax: 01884 243325
email: sales@halsgrove.com
website: www.halsgrove.com

ACKNOWLEDGEMENTS
With thanks to The National Trust at Flatford Mill, Ickworth House,
Lavenham Guildhall of Corpus Christi and Dunwich Heath.

Printed and bound D'Auria Industrie Grafiche Spa, Italy

INTRODUCTION

The variety of landscapes contained within Suffolk's borders is quite astounding – from its pastoral river valley landscape to the south, through its agricultural heart with huge skies, to the north which has its own blend of fenland in the west through forest, heath and broadland, to the coast in the east. And the coast is truly very special indeed, boasting the most easterly point in the UK, the largest shingle spit in Europe and one of its busiest container ports, plus wonderfully peaceful stretches of wild shifting coastline, dotted along its length with elegant seaside towns and old fishing hamlets.

Take a little time to investigate and you will find that the rich and varied history of Suffolk has played a key role in the development of the world far beyond the county's borders.

From ancient settlements and invasion by Vikings through to early royal castles and baronial power struggles. From huge wealth and prosperity generated by the medieval woollen-cloth trade to the disaster of the Black Death. From top-secret pioneering work in times of war to world-class research and development in peace time. From a snarling red-eyed hound from hell to visitors from outer-space. All in all, it is a county with more than just a few stories to tell…

Great charm is added to the county by virtue of its very own dialect which lives on through colloquial turns of phrase, and through the pronunciation of many different place names. The people are genuinely friendly, possessing a generosity of spirit that seems to have deserted many other places in the twenty-first century – whilst photographing the rising sun from a roadside very early one morning, all three of the drivers who passed stopped to offer assistance, thinking I may have broken down.

In this book I have tried to capture and portray the essence of the county as I have seen it – many of the subjects have been photographed around sunrise or sunset when the light is at its best for landscape photography. A firm believer that landscapes are the sum of their parts, I have also included a number of intimate, close-up photographs of subjects that I have seen in my travels.

Although far from being a stranger to Suffolk, I have truly enjoyed travelling around and fully exploring the county. I hope that it will inspire visitors to take a closer look at what this beautiful and varied place has to offer, and serve to remind those lucky enough to reside there of what a truly wonderful area it is that they call home.

David Gynn
enquiries@stourvalleyphotography.com

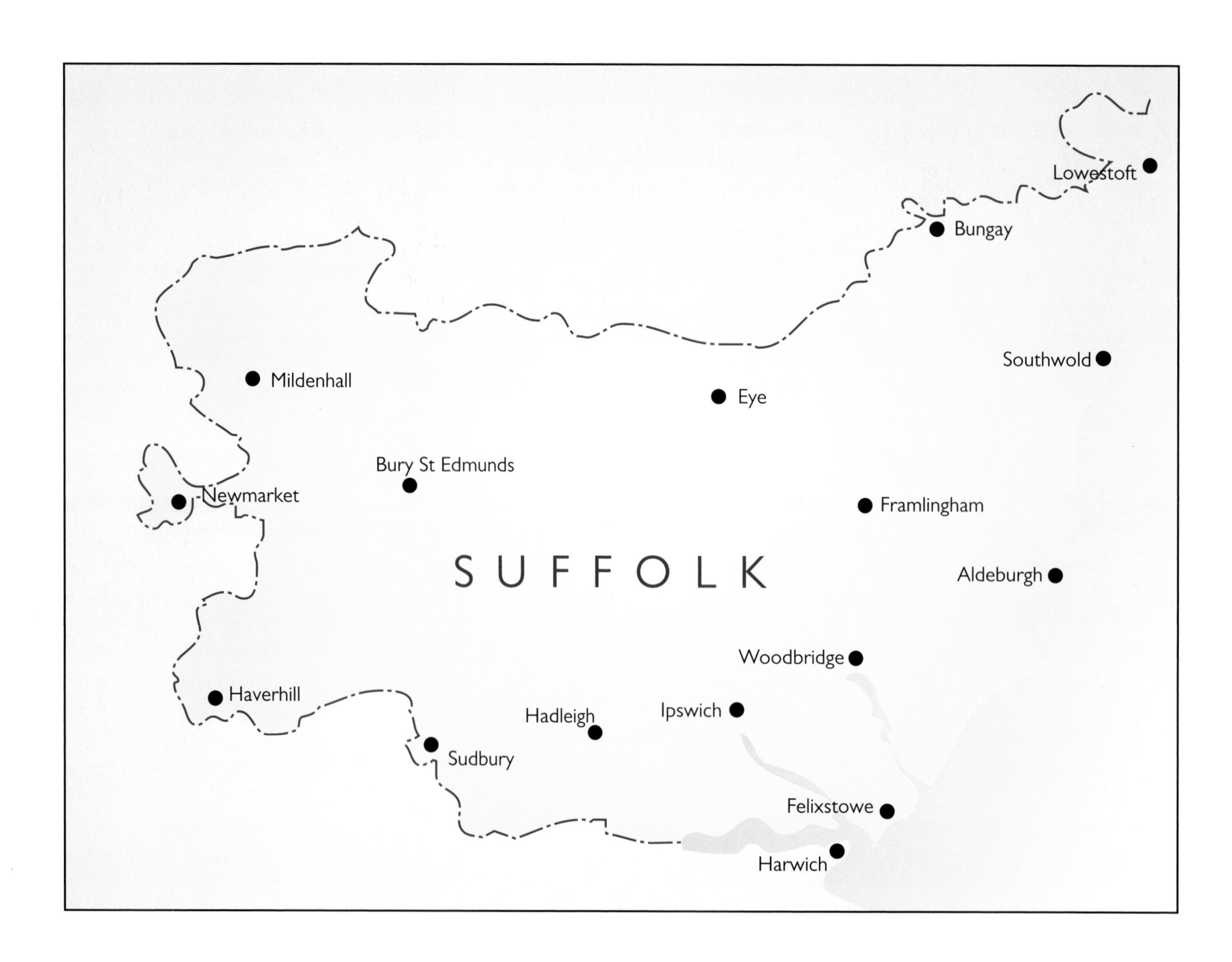

Lowestoft
Bungay
Southwold
Mildenhall
Eye
Bury St Edmunds
Newmarket
Framlingham
SUFFOLK
Aldeburgh
Woodbridge
Haverhill
Hadleigh
Ipswich
Sudbury
Felixstowe
Harwich

Monks Eleigh – one of Suffolk's many picturesque villages.

Buttercups carpeting a flood meadow in summer.

The dense and prickly gorse with its bright yellow flowers is a common sight in coastal and heathland areas in the east of the county.

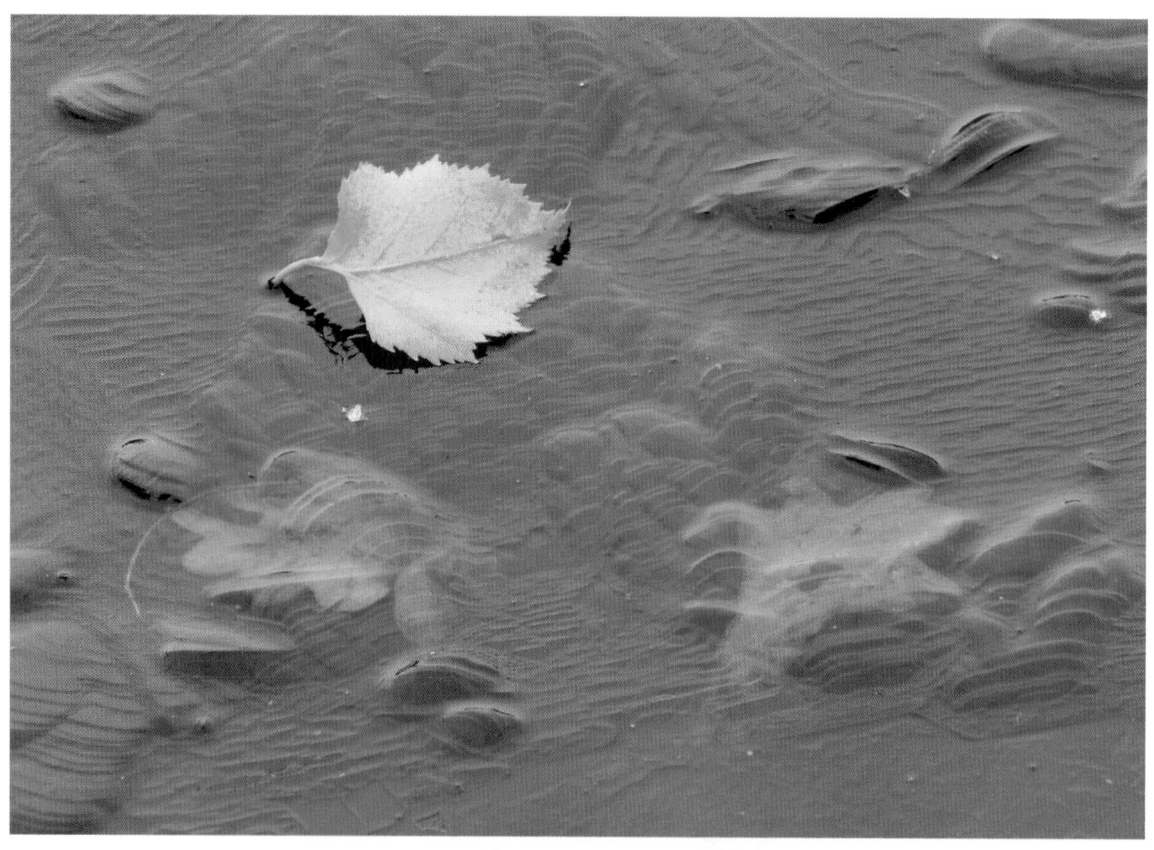

Leaves are trapped beneath the ice, while a newly fallen birch leaf sits on top of the frozen pond.

A stranded tree on the beach at Benacre, evidence of continuous erosion and change to the coastline. Erosion of the cliffs along this part of the Suffolk coast also reveals the occasional glacial fossil.

The wide swathes of shingle beaches along the Suffolk coast are surprisingly well inhabited by plants, such as this yellow horned poppy, which offer displays of colour that are unexpected in such an unforgiving landscape.

A vast deserted beach is enjoyed by a lone walker soon after sunrise.

Leiston Abbey now houses the National School for Young Chamber Music Players. Dating from 1362, it retains an unusual blend of Norman and Gothic details, and is an imposing sight when first glimpsed across rolling fields.

The beach at Walberswick, wide, gently sloping and sandy – with just a little shingle in evidence along the tidal range.

Easily recognised as the house in John Constable's painting 'The Haywain' of nearly 200 years ago, Willy Lott's House at Flatford sits across the millstream, gently softened by early morning mist.

Not all windmills have survived replacement with newer methods – although at least this derelict shell is still making its mark on the landscape, unlike a great many that have disappeared forever.

Snape Maltings provides a special setting for a range of unique shops and galleries, plus the world famous concert hall.

Said to be one of England's most significant medieval buildings, few people can have failed to marvel at the spectacular church of the Most Holy Trinity as they have driven through the village of Blythburgh. In a county of so many beautiful churches, this is considered by many to be the very best.

New life abounds in spring in the woods and forests. It's hard to imagine this tiny fern in a bed of moss growing to the size it will reach in the few short weeks till autumn.

Bluebells herald a new season and new life among decay on the floor of one of Suffolk's numerous woodland and forest areas.

Lavenham – famous as the county's best kept small Tudor town – is full of the magnificent former dwellings of the rich woollen-cloth merchants who lived in this once single-industry town.

The River Stour in Constable Country and its ever popular rowing boats – some even equipped with their own tow-along duck for the amusement of children.

A crisp and frosty start to a new day at Thelnetham's working conically-capped windmill dating from 1819.

In the north-west corner of Suffolk the landscape changes completely, from forest and heathland to the starkness of the fens. It's flat, with arrow-straight roads and drainage ditches, few trees apart from those forming wind-breaks or sheltering small houses and farms, and the soil is rich and peaty.

A glimpse of the impressive Framlingham Castle. Built as his stronghold by the rebellious Earl of Norfolk late in the twelfth century, this was where Mary was proclaimed Queen in 1553.

Pleasure craft moored on Oulton Broad – ready for another lovely day on these inland waters.

Farming implements add interest to countless views in the agricultural heart of the county.

Nestled serenely into the landscape of the River Gipping near Ipswich, the existing Sproughton Mill dates from 1818.

A late afternoon view across one of south Suffolk's valleys in autumn – a quiet, pastoral delight.

A footpath is devoid of walkers on a day when the interesting light is frequently interrupted by 'stair-rod' rain.

A view across the tranquil flood meadows at Sudbury towards pretty painted cottages.

Suffolk exhibits a wide range of landscapes, including some wonderfully gentle rolling countryside around its various river valleys such as here in the Brett valley.

The Italianate Ickworth House of 1795, with its tremendously imposing oval rotunda and curved wings, was built by the famously eccentric 4th Earl of Bristol to house a collection of treasures from around Europe. Owned by the National Trust, today it houses an important collection of 'old masters' and has fabulous gardens and walks through the 1800 acres of parkland.

St Mary's Church at East Bergholt, a stunning but unfinished building where construction of the tower ceased with the onset of the Reformation. The church's peal of five bells – the heaviest in the world – is installed in what was probably designed as a temporary bell cage in 1531, from where the bells still ring today.

Cattle enjoying the waters of the River Stour at Sudbury – the Highland cattle are among the more unusual residents of pastures in Suffolk.

Herringfleet smock mill, a fabulously restored example of what was once one of many wind-pumps used to drain marshland into the rivers – in this case the River Waveney.

Bridge Cottage and the bridge at Flatford – early on a rare but beautiful snowy winter morning.

Stoke-by-Nayland's St Mary's Church can be seen for many miles around. The range of impressive timbered buildings in the village is a reminder of the great wealth that the wool trade brought to the area during the middle ages.

The beach at Aldeburgh is famed for its small fleet of fishing boats, the associated paraphernalia and for the fishermen's huts from where the fresh catch can be purchased.

Port of Felixstowe
MSC LORETTA
PANAMA

Since it was founded in 1875, Felixstowe Dock has continued to grow to meet the demands placed upon it. Here we see some of the massive container ships that frequent the port with just a few of the incredible one million containers handled by the port each year.

The landscape around Hundon demonstrates why Suffolk is renowned for having huge skies.

Autumn means spectacular displays of colour under the skies of Suffolk.

Dating from 1165, the remains of King Henry II's Orford Castle make for a truly impressive sight – even though much of the original castle is long gone. It was built to protect against invasion from the sea and to assert authority over the region.

Southwold – a truly elegant traditional seaside resort famed for its beach and huts and also for its splendid architecture, lighthouse and brewery.

Two of the facets of Lowestoft's marine heritage are seen here – to the left the town's yacht marina and to the right a large specialised rig tender returns under the town's lifting road bridge.

Suffolk's landscapes are varied indeed. Oulton Broad forms the southern edge to the Broads National Park – more typically associated with neighbouring Norfolk. In 1956 Oulton Broad saw Sir Christopher Cockerell test the world's first working model of a hovercraft.

Modern beach huts on the promenade at Lowestoft look very crisp and well organised with their rhythmic pattern of coloured doors.

Mid-Suffolk is justly famed for its many pretty villages. This is a view of Rattlesden with its timbered houses and St Nicolas's Church perched in an elevated position in the Rat valley.

The impressive landmark of St Peter and St Paul's at Lavenham was built with 'new money' in the woollen-cloth-rich days of the 1530s. The sharp lines are in distinct contrast to the twisted, warped, leaning nature of nearly every other building in this famously well-preserved Tudor town.

By the side of the road and the very edge of Thetford Forest Park stands Suffolk's tallest memorial, to the war dead of the three surrounding parishes of Elveden, Eriswell and Icklingham.

Overnight snow hangs briefly in the branches before it is thawed by the gentle winter sun.

Dating from 1751, the beautifully restored Stanton Post Mill is in full working condition. It is one of only seven remaining out of some three hundred post mills that existed in the county at the beginning of the nineteenth century.

A view across the frozen man-made 'Meare' at Thorpeness. This former fishing hamlet was re-created as an early-twentieth-century middle-class seaside resort with a Peter Pan theme.

This weathered old hawthorn in a flood meadow has dry feet – for now.

Lowestoft's Ness Point – the most easterly point in the United Kingdom. The place marker resembles a compass with indications of the directions and distances to towns around the world.

Early morning dew enhances the magic of a spider's web.

With so much water in the landscape, Suffolk is home to many kinds of water loving wildlife – here a young family of Canada Geese.

Woodbridge on the River Deben is popular with visitors from both land and sea. The Tide Mill, seen here in the background, was built in 1793 and is a local architectural icon.

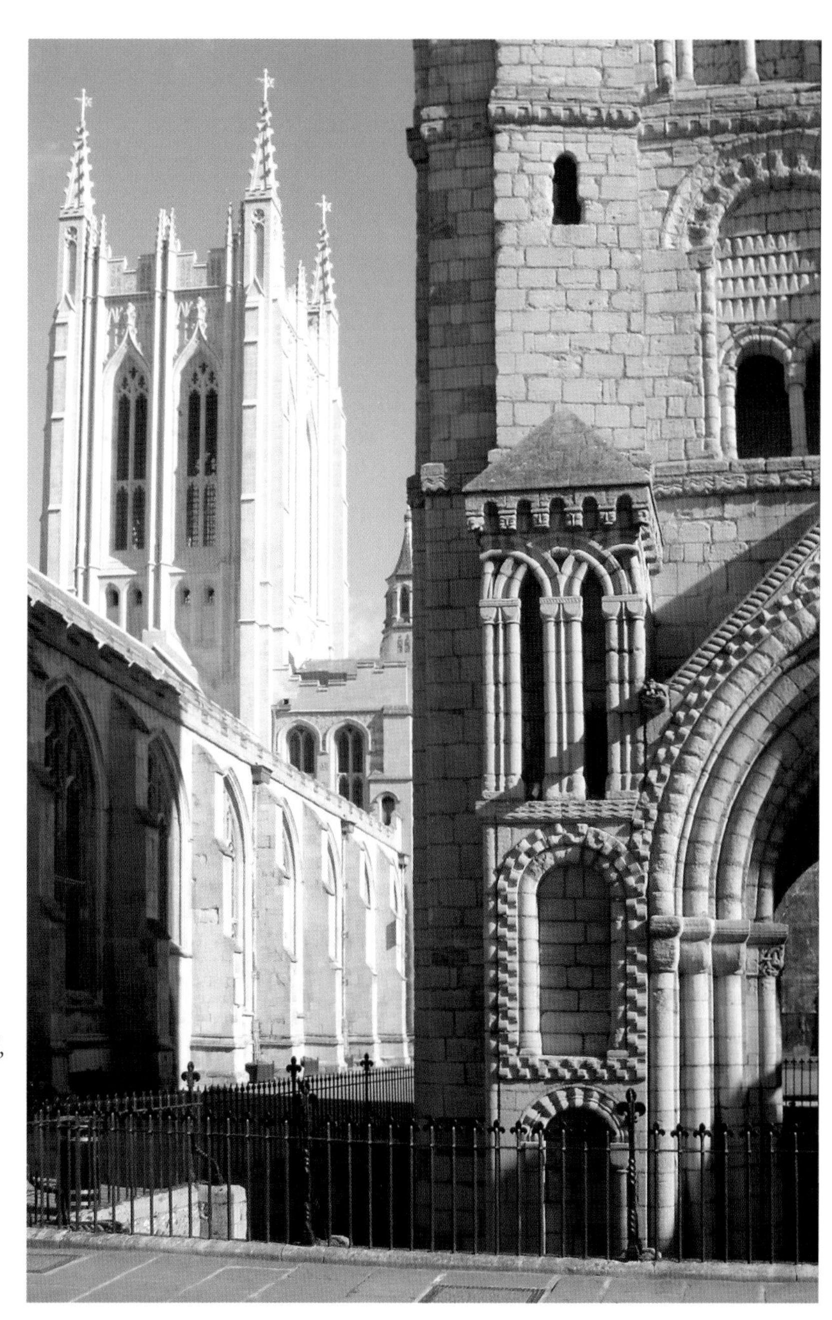

Construction started on St James' Church in Bury St Edmunds, a pilgrimage site to the martyred King Edmund, in 1503. The church became St Edmundsbury Cathedral in 1914 and work to erect the tower, seen gleaming in the sunshine, was completed in 2005.

Rebuilt, restored and re-opened in 2001 Southwold Pier houses an interesting collection of unique home-made slot-machines and simulator rides by engineer and cartoonist Tim Hunkin.

In winter all the detail of the branch and twig skeletons is revealed along this field boundary hedgerow.

In the north of the county is the small market town of Eye, named from the old English word for island when it was surrounded by the waters of the River Dove and various marshes. Containing a number of impressive buildings, Eye was once of great strategic importance.

The setting sun dips behind the trees on a misty afternoon near Woodbridge.

With the North Sea, rivers, estuaries, broads, meres and drainage channels – water is never far away in Suffolk.

The ancient Buttercross in the attractive market town of Bungay, where St Mary's Church (as folklore would have it) was attacked in 1577 by East Anglia's legendary snarling hound from hell – Black Shuck.

All manner of interesting detail and texture can be seen on Suffolk's beaches.

The impressive arc of the Orwell Bridge at Ipswich. When the bridge was finished in 1982 its central span was the longest pre-stressed concrete span in the world.

A threatening sky out to sea warns of approaching rain.

Old timbers on the beach at Bawdsey take a pounding from crashing waves driven by a north-easterly gale.

Dunwich Heath is one of Suffolk's most important nature conservation areas and surely one of its most beautiful. Over 200 acres of flowering heather and gorse, sandy cliffs and a shingle beach mean that Dunwich Heath is a truly wonderful place for a walk.

Willy Lott's House and the frozen millstream at Flatford after a cold and snowy winter night.

Heather and gorse at Dunwich Heath, up close and prickly!

Colourful beach huts, with their amusing names and high price tags, are one of Southwold's many claims to fame.

Foxgloves provide summer colour and architectural splendour to open areas of woodland and hedgerows.

With its immaculate village green, pastel painted cottages, inns and fabulous church, Cavendish still shows that it was a place of great wealth in the middle ages.

Pigs play a major part in Suffolk farming – large pig villages are now quite a common sight.

The magnificent Scallop Shell on the beach at Aldeburgh, a memorial to Benjamin Britten by Maggi Hambling. Seen here it is reflecting the rich hues of the sky and rising sun, long before breakfast in mid-summer.

Established in 1248, Clare Priory is one of the oldest religious houses in England and the building itself dates from the fourteenth century. It sits over the River Stour from the medieval village of Clare, with its ruined castle and wonderful old houses.

The clouds are coloured and the promenade buildings softly lit by the low angle of the rising sun.

The late spring blue carpeting of a woodland floor is broken only by the occasional white bluebell.

The Stour Valley Path, a 60 mile footpath from Newmarket to Cattawade, provides a treat during the early summer months – the Pasque Flower. This beautiful flower is a rare sight and the awe-inspiring, ancient earthworks of Devil's Dyke is one of the few places in the UK where it can be seen.

The village sign at Blythburgh.

The Guildhall of Corpus Christi in the market place at Lavenham was built in about 1530, and was at the centre of the town's woollen-cloth merchant business which brought huge wealth. After the Reformation, however, it saw less glamorous uses as town hall, prison, then workhouse before being restored to the remarkable building that it is today.

The magnificent windmill at Pakenham – Suffolk's only village to boast both a windmill and a watermill. Although the windmill no longer works, the sails can sometimes be seen turning.

A bright, frosty start to the day in north Suffolk.

Built for an altogether more genteel age, these former beach changing rooms at Lowestoft have been converted into interesting beach huts.

The large swaying flowers of oxeye daisies can be seen in fields and dotted along roadsides all over the county in summer.

Wind and waves mean that some of the fishermen's huts dotted along the Suffolk coast have developed a character all of their own.

The fine mill at Bures bathed in the rays of the afternoon sun – just ahead of the approaching storm clouds.

At the right time of year, areas of woodland resemble shimmering lakes, created by the seed-heads of honesty.

A boardwalk to the beach at Sizewell is highlighted by a dusting of snow in early morning sunlight.

At the western end of the River Stour's role as the Essex/Suffolk border near Haverhill lies Baythorne Mill.

The surf, beach and cliffs of Benacre Beach.

Dawn across fields from a country lane in the north of the county.

Thorpeness in winter – and the usually shifting shingle beach is frozen solid under foot. The beach houses here have a fabulous view of the sun rising out over the sea but are first in line to deal with the ravages of winter storms.

In Newmarket you're never far from the 'Sport of Kings'. After the jockeys have put them through their paces out on the gallops, the racehorses make a slow walk back into the heart of the town on a chilly winter morning.

*More latterly famous for its power station, Sizewell also has a long history as a fishing hamlet.
Evidence of this can be seen along its shingle beach which remains very popular with beach fisherman today.*

A newly-born calf gets reassuring attention from its mother.

In the fens, as elsewhere in agricultural Suffolk, various pieces of farm machinery – old and new – provide interest and context to the landscape.

Woodland walks provide a very pleasant and interesting way to spend time in Suffolk.

Nestling in the Brett valley with its lovely timbered buildings and quaint ford, Kersey is a fine example of a Suffolk community that benefited greatly from wool wealth.

Many of Suffolk's steep shingle beaches contain a fascinating array of different winches used to haul fishing boats from the waves.

Kentwell Hall at Long Melford is probably England's finest example of a moated Tudor house – built like so many of the impressive buildings in the area on woollen-cloth wealth. Approached along its impressive ¾ mile avenue of lime trees, and now famous for its Tudor and Second World War re-creation days, Kentwell Hall provides an opportunity to glimpse a long-gone era.

Poppies lit from behind – showing the delicacy of the fragile petals.

Coastal erosion reveals the strata of sand and shingle which form the dunes – the backdrop to the beach at Walberswick.

Fungi of all shapes, sizes and colours can add to the interest of an autumnal walk. This is a stunning but poisonous fly agaric.

Detail from the forest floor at Tunstall Forest in autumn.

Suffolk's coast has long been popular with visitors. The pier at Felixstowe was originally more than 800 yards long when it was built in 1905 for the berthing of steamers, trade that soon succumbed to the railways. Now less than a quarter remains.

Down by the protected waters of the River Blyth in Walberswick there is a picturesque small community of fishermen's huts.

The magnificent bronze statue of Hyperion, winner of the 1933 Derby, stands proudly outside the Jockey Club in Newmarket – the historical home of British horseracing.

The town of Aldeburgh sits right on the edge of its wide and steep shingle beach.

Old steelwork slowly rusts away while the beach changes shape around it and nature takes over.

Flatford Mill and millpond after heavy rain in late summer – for a short while the typically calm millpond is a rush of moving water.

One of many cranes at Felixstowe's Landguard Dock, part of the UK's largest container port.

At Shingle Street, as elsewhere, the beach is in a constant state of change. Even the quite gentle waves pictured have the power to throw yet more stones on to the beach.

Shingle Street's Coastguard cottages seen across the vast expanse of beach – a remarkably wild and remote place about which wartime secrets and myths still abound.

Detail of shingle, pebbles and sea-worn driftwood on a Suffolk beach.

The sun rises out beyond Southwold Pier – voted 'Pier of the Year' in 2002 this is surely the most elegant pier on the east coast. When it was built in 1900 the pier was 810ft long, but it has seen plenty of suffering, the final blow reducing it to just 150ft after a storm in 1979. Now fully restored, it was re-opened by the Duke of Gloucester in 2001.

The rising winter sun warms the ancient pollarded willows – and a particularly sociable mallard – on the River Stour.

St Mary's Church, Stoke-by-Nayland, and fading leaves are warmed by the first golden rays on an autumn morning.

One of Suffolk's small fishing boats makes an early start.

The massive and varied patchwork of Thetford Forest Park straddles the Suffolk/Norfolk border. The acute angle of the rising sun gives shape and form to the trees of The King's Forest that is lost once the sun is above the canopy.

River reflections on a bracing winter morning.

The River Stour meanders quietly along the Essex/Suffolk border.

Sunrise, spectacularly coloured through a low sea-mist.

The sun rises from behind one of north Suffolk's many woodland areas, close to the Norfolk border and Thetford Forest.

Frost picks out the lines of a young seedling crop at sunrise on a cold day in early winter.

Flood meadow mists along the River Stour are fleetingly turned orange by the rising sun.

Old wind-twisted trees are a distinct feature of the Suffolk landscape – the ones seen here at sunset are near Covehithe.

Dawn on Suffolk's 'Sunrise Coast.'

A view down the River Deben towards the setting sun.

Flood meadows can be fabulously damp and misty places early on summer mornings.

A small fishing boat makes headway through the waves off the 'Sunrise Coast'.

Fishing boat detail on the beach at Aldeburgh.

A bold advertisement on the billiard table landscape of the fens.

Sunlight and warmth soon cut through early morning mist.

Fungi spring up among the fallen leaves in Rendlesham Forest.

Freshly fallen onto a bed of frosted leaves, it's easy to imagine this chestnut leaf drifting down from its branch in the cold of the night.

St Andrew's Church at Covehithe is an incredible place to behold. Once one of three large churches in the area, most of the original building survives only as a spectacular ruin – a later and far smaller church stands within the remains.

The sun appears on the horizon out beyond the harbour wall at Lowestoft.